Savoring Okra Delights
A Culinary Journey through Irresistible Okra Soup with Succulent Meat Pieces

While every precaution has been taken in the preparation of this book, the publisher assumes no responsibility for errors or omissions, or for damages resulting from the use of the information contained herein.

SAVORING OKRA DELIGHTS

First edition. February 4, 2024.

Copyright © 2024 Jose Maria.

ISBN: 979-8223466925

Written by Jose Maria.

Table of Contents

Jose Maria

❖ Introduction

A. Welcome and Overview

Welcome to a culinary exploration that promises to tickle your taste buds and introduce you to the world of Okra Soup with Succulent Meat Pieces. This journey is not just about preparing a meal; it's an invitation to savor the rich flavors and cultural significance embedded in every spoonful of this delectable dish.

As you embark on this culinary adventure, let the tantalizing aroma of fresh okra and succulent meat guide you through a delightful cooking experience. Whether you're a seasoned chef or a kitchen novice, this recipe is crafted to be both accessible and rewarding.

B. History and Significance of Okra Soup

Before we dive into the pots and pans, let's take a moment to appreciate the history and cultural significance of Okra Soup. Originating from West Africa, this soup has traversed continents and found a place in the hearts of many cuisines.

Okra, known for its unique texture and mild flavor, serves as the star ingredient in this dish. Its journey in the culinary world reflects the diversity of tastes and the way different regions have embraced and personalized this recipe.

In various cultures, Okra Soup symbolizes warmth, togetherness, and celebration. It's a dish that brings families and communities together, with its roots deeply embedded in shared meals and cherished traditions.

As we venture into the kitchen, let's carry with us not just the ingredients but also the stories and traditions that make Okra Soup a truly special and beloved dish. Get ready to create memories and savor the irresistible delights that await you in every bowl.

Chapter (1) Getting Started

A. Ingredients

1. Fresh Okra: Begin with approximately 1 pound of fresh okra. Look for vibrant green pods, avoiding any that are overly mature or tough.

2. Meat Selection (Chicken, Beef, or Lamb): Choose your preferred meat for a hearty infusion of flavor. Whether it's succulent chicken, robust beef, or tender lamb, select around 1.5 pounds, ensuring it's cut into bite-sized pieces for easy integration into the soup.

3. Aromatics (Onions, Garlic, Ginger): Build a flavorful base with 1 large onion, finely chopped, 3 cloves of garlic minced, and a thumb-sized piece of ginger, grated.

4. Spices and Herbs (Bay Leaves, Thyme, Parsley): Add depth with 2 bay leaves, 1 teaspoon of dried thyme, and a handful of fresh parsley, chopped.

5. Broth or Stock: Enhance the soup's richness with 6 cups of your preferred broth or stock, be it vegetable, chicken, or beef.

6. Tomatoes and Tomato Paste: Introduce a tomato-based richness with 2 large tomatoes, diced, and 2 tablespoons of tomato paste.

7. Additional Flavor Enhancements (optional): Feel free to personalize with optional additions such as 1 teaspoon of paprika for a subtle smokiness or a pinch of red pepper flakes for a hint of heat.

B. Kitchen Tools and Equipment

1. Large Pot: Ensure you have a spacious pot to accommodate the soup. A 6 to 8-quart pot works well.

2. Cutting Board and Knife: Prepare a sturdy cutting board and a sharp knife for chopping and slicing your ingredients.
3. Ladle or Spoon: Have a ladle or a large spoon on hand for easy serving and stirring.
4. Blender (optional): While not mandatory, having a blender can aid in achieving a smoother consistency if desired.

Chapter (2) Preparing Okra

A. Cleaning and Slicing Techniques

Cleaning Okra:

Begin by rinsing the okra under cold water to remove any dirt or debris.

Pat the okra dry with a clean kitchen towel.

Slicing Okra:

Trim off the stem ends of the okra pods.

Depending on your preference, slice the okra into rounds or lengthwise into halves. Aim for uniform pieces to ensure even cooking.

B. Tips for Reducing Okra's Sliminess

Okra is notorious for its natural sliminess, but fear not – there are effective ways to minimize it in your soup:

Pre-soaking Okra:

To reduce sliminess, soak the sliced okra in vinegar or lemon juice for about 30 minutes before cooking.

Drain and rinse the okra thoroughly to remove the vinegar or lemon juice.

Dry Okra Completely:

Ensure that the okra is completely dry before slicing and adding it to the pot. Excess moisture can contribute to sliminess.

High Heat Cooking:

Cooking okra over high heat can help reduce sliminess. Searing or roasting the okra before incorporating it into the soup can enhance its texture.

Acidic Ingredients:

Incorporating acidic ingredients like tomatoes or a splash of lime juice can help counteract the sliminess of okra.

By following these techniques, you'll not only prepare the okra for the soup but also mitigate its characteristic sliminess, resulting in a more enjoyable dining experience.

Chapter (3) Meat Preparations

A. Choosing the Right Cuts

Consider Your Preference:

Select meat cuts based on your preference, whether it's the tenderness of chicken, the richness of beef, or the unique flavor of lamb.

For chicken, boneless, skinless thighs or breasts work well. For beef or lamb, opt for stewing cuts with a good balance of lean meat and marbling.

Bite-Sized Pieces:

Cube the chosen meat into bite-sized pieces, ensuring uniformity for even cooking and a delightful dining experience.

B. Marinating Options

Flavorful Base:

Create a marinade using a mixture of olive oil, minced garlic, chopped parsley, a pinch of salt, and black pepper.

Allow the meat to marinate for at least 30 minutes to infuse it with flavor.

Customization:

Feel free to customize the marinade with additional herbs or spices to complement the overall profile of the dish.

C. Cooking Techniques (Boiling, Grilling, or Roasting)

Boiling:

Simmer the marinated meat in a pot of water until it reaches a tender and succulent consistency.

Reserve the broth for later use in the soup.

Grilling or Roasting (Optional):

For added depth of flavor, consider grilling or roasting the marinated meat until it develops a savory crust.

This step is optional but can impart a delightful smokiness to the overall dish.

D. Slicing and Shredding for Soup Integration

Uniform Slices:

Once the meat is cooked, slice it into uniform pieces. For chicken, consider shredding it into bite-sized strands.

Ready for Integration:

Your marinated and cooked meat is now ready to be integrated into the soup, providing a hearty and flavorful component.

With these carefully chosen cuts, marination, and cooking techniques, the meat will add a savory depth to your Okra Soup, making each spoonful a satisfying experience.

Chapter (4) Base Preparation

A. Sauteing Aromatics

Heating the Pot:

Place a large pot over medium heat and add a drizzle of oil.

Once the oil is heated, add the finely chopped onions, minced garlic, and grated ginger.

Sweating Aromatics:

Saute the aromatics until the onions become translucent and a fragrant aroma fills the kitchen.

B. Incorporating Tomatoes and Tomato Paste

Tomato Addition:

Introduce the diced tomatoes to the pot, stirring well to combine with the sauteed aromatics.

Allow the tomatoes to cook down until they release their juices and form a thick base.

Tomato Paste Boost:

Stir in the tomato paste, ensuring it's well distributed to enhance the soup's richness.

Let the mixture simmer for a few minutes, allowing the flavors to meld.

C. Adding Spices and Herbs for Depth of Flavor

Layering Flavors:

Drop in the bay leaves, dried thyme, and the fresh parsley, stirring to infuse the base with aromatic herbs.

Adjust the heat to medium-low to avoid scorching the herbs.

Customizing Spices:

Feel free to tailor the spice levels to your preference. Add a pinch of red pepper flakes for heat or a teaspoon of paprika for a subtle smokiness.

D. Creating a Flavorful Broth

Pouring Broth:

Gradually pour in the preferred broth or stock, stirring continuously to combine the ingredients into a cohesive base.

Scrape any flavorful bits from the bottom of the pot to incorporate into the broth.

Bringing to a Simmer:

Allow the broth to come to a gentle simmer, letting the flavors meld and the base reach a savory depth.

By meticulously sautéing aromatics, incorporating tomatoes, adding a variety of spices and herbs, and creating a flavorful broth, you are laying the foundation for an Okra Soup that is rich in taste and character.

Chapter (5) Bringing It All Together

A. Combining Okra and Meat

Integrating Okra:

Carefully add the prepared okra to the simmering broth, ensuring an even distribution.

Stir gently to combine, allowing the okra to absorb the rich flavors of the base.

Adding Cooked Meat:

Introduce the sliced or shredded, cooked meat to the pot, allowing it to merge seamlessly with the okra and broth.

Stir gently to ensure all components are well-incorporated.

B. Adjusting Seasonings to Taste

Taste Testing:

Take a moment to taste the soup and adjust the seasoning. Add salt and pepper as needed to achieve a perfectly balanced flavor profile.

Balancing Flavors:

Consider additional herbs or spices to elevate the taste. A dash of fresh parsley or a sprinkle of thyme can enhance the aromatic bouquet.

C. Simmering for Optimal Flavor Fusion

Gentle Simmer:

Allow the soup to simmer over medium-low heat, giving the ingredients time to meld and the flavors to harmonize.

Cover the pot partially, allowing steam to escape while maintaining the simmer.

Patience for Perfection:

Simmer the soup for at least 30-45 minutes, allowing the okra and meat to absorb the rich flavors of the broth.

Adjust Consistency if Needed:

If the soup appears too thick, you can add additional broth or water to reach your desired consistency.

By bringing together the okra, meat, and meticulously prepared base, you're setting the stage for a soup that captures the essence of each ingredient. As the flavors meld through gentle simmering, prepare to indulge in a bowl of Okra Soup that embodies the warmth and depth of this culinary journey.

Chapter (6) Serving Suggestions

A. Accompanying Side Dishes (Rice, Fufu, Bread)

Rice:

Serve your Okra Soup over a bed of steamed white rice for a classic pairing. The rice will absorb the flavorful broth, creating a satisfying and hearty meal.

Fufu:

For an authentic experience, pair the soup with fufu, a starchy side dish popular in West African cuisine. Fufu's mild taste complements the robust flavors of the soup.

Bread:

Crusty bread or warm dinner rolls are excellent for dipping into the savory broth. The contrast in texture adds a delightful element to the dining experience.

B. Garnishing for Presentation

Fresh Herbs:

Sprinkle freshly chopped parsley or cilantro over the soup just before serving. The vibrant greens add a burst of freshness and visual appeal.

Lemon or Lime Wedges:

Provide lemon or lime wedges on the side. Squeezing a bit of citrus over the soup just before eating can brighten the flavors.

Dollop of Yogurt or Sour Cream (Optional):

For a creamy touch, add a dollop of plain yogurt or sour cream. The coolness balances the warmth of the soup.

C. Beverage Pairings (Suggested drinks)

Hibiscus Tea:

The floral and slightly tart notes of hibiscus tea complement the richness of the soup.

Light White Wine:

Consider serving a light and crisp white wine, such as Sauvignon Blanc or Pinot Grigio, to enhance the dining experience.

Citrus-Infused Water:

Create a refreshing citrus-infused water with slices of oranges, lemons, and limes for a non-alcoholic option.

Ginger Beer:

The zesty kick of ginger beer pairs well with the warmth of the spices in the soup.

These serving suggestions aim to elevate your Okra Soup experience, providing a variety of options to suit different tastes and preferences. Enjoy the symphony of flavors and textures as you savor each spoonful of this delightful dish.

Chapter (7) Variations and Customizations

A. Vegetarian/Vegan Options

Vegetarian Okra Soup:

Substitute the meat with plant-based proteins such as tofu, tempeh, or chickpeas. Ensure the broth is vegetable-based, and consider adding extra vegetables like carrots or bell peppers for texture and flavor.

Vegan Twist:

To make the soup entirely vegan, avoid animal-derived ingredients. Use vegetable broth, and ensure any optional flavor enhancements are plant-based.

B. Regional Twists on Okra Soup

West African Style:

Embrace the traditional West African preparation by incorporating ingredients like ground crayfish, palm oil, or traditional seasonings specific to the region.

Caribbean Fusion:

Add a Caribbean twist with coconut milk for a rich and creamy variation. Include Caribbean spices like allspice or Scotch bonnet peppers for a flavorful kick.

Mediterranean Flair:

Infuse Mediterranean flavors by adding olives, capers, and a splash of lemon. Consider using Mediterranean herbs such as oregano and rosemary.

C. Health-Conscious Adjustments

Lean Protein Choices:

Opt for lean protein sources like skinless chicken breast, lean beef, or lean cuts of lamb to reduce overall fat content.

Whole Grain Options:

Substitute white rice with brown rice or quinoa for added fiber and nutritional benefits.

Reduced Sodium Broth:

Use low-sodium or homemade broth to control the salt content. Adjust salt levels during seasoning to taste.

Additional Vegetables:

Boost the nutritional content by adding more vegetables such as spinach, kale, or okra varieties.

These variations cater to different dietary preferences and allow you to customize the Okra Soup to suit your taste or explore diverse regional adaptations. Feel free to experiment and make the dish uniquely yours.

Chapter (8) Troubleshooting

A. Dealing with Sliminess

Pre-soaking Techniques:

If the okra imparts more sliminess than desired, try pre-soaking it in vinegar or lemon juice for an extended period before cooking.

Ensure the okra is thoroughly dried after soaking to prevent excess moisture.

Cooking Methods:

Searing or roasting the okra before adding it to the soup can help minimize sliminess.

Cooking the okra over high heat and avoiding overcooking can also reduce its slimy texture.

Acidic Ingredients:

Incorporating acidic elements like tomatoes or a splash of lime juice not only adds flavor but also helps counteract the sliminess.

B. Adjusting Spice Levels

Taste and Adjust:

If the spice levels are too mild or intense, taste the soup and adjust accordingly.

To decrease heat, consider adding a small amount of sweetness, such as a teaspoon of honey or sugar.

To increase heat, add a pinch of cayenne pepper or red pepper flakes.

Balancing Flavors:

If the soup seems too spicy, balance the flavors by adding more broth or coconut milk (if applicable) to dilute the spice.

C. Modifying for Dietary Restrictions

Gluten-Free Options:

Ensure all ingredients, including spices and broths, are gluten-free if needed. Substitute traditional flour for gluten-free alternatives for thickening if necessary.

Dairy-Free Adaptations:

For dairy-free versions, skip any dairy-based garnishes and ensure that the broth and flavor enhancements are free from dairy components.

Low-Carb Adjustments:

To reduce the carbohydrate content, minimize starchy side dishes like rice or fufu. Focus on the protein and vegetable elements of the soup.

Allergen Considerations:

Always check ingredient labels for potential allergens and choose substitutions accordingly. For example, use soy or almond milk as a dairy alternative.

By addressing common issues like sliminess and providing guidance on adjusting spice levels and modifying for dietary restrictions, you can ensure that your Okra Soup meets your preferences and dietary needs.

Chapter (9) Tips and Tricks

A. Time-Saving Hacks

Prep in Advance:

Chop and marinate the meat, clean and slice the okra, and prepare aromatics ahead of time for quicker assembly when cooking.

Frozen Okra:

Consider using frozen okra as a time-saving option. It's pre-sliced and retains a good texture when added to the soup.

Store-Bought Broth:

If time is limited, opt for high-quality store-bought broth to save time on preparing homemade broth.

B. Storage and Reheating Suggestions

Refrigeration:

Store leftover Okra Soup in airtight containers in the refrigerator for up to 3-4 days.

Freezing:

Okra Soup freezes well. Portion it into freezer-safe containers, leaving room for expansion, and store for up to 2-3 months.

Reheating:

When reheating, add a splash of broth or water to maintain the soup's consistency.

Reheat on the stove over medium heat, stirring occasionally until warmed through.

C. Flavor-Enhancing Secrets

Fresh Herbs at the End:

Add a handful of fresh herbs, like cilantro or parsley, just before serving for a burst of fresh flavor.

Citrus Zest:

Enhance the soup's brightness by adding a touch of citrus zest (lemon or lime) right before serving.

Finish with a Drizzle:

Drizzle a high-quality olive oil over individual servings just before serving to add richness and depth.

Umami Boosters:

Enhance the umami profile with a dash of soy sauce or Worcestershire sauce, adding complexity to the flavor.

By incorporating time-saving hacks, ensuring proper storage and reheating, and implementing flavor-enhancing secrets, you can make the Okra Soup experience more convenient and elevate its taste to new heights.

Chapter (10) Okra Varieties and Seasonal Considerations

A. Exploring Different Okra Types

Traditional Green Okra:

The most common variety, known for its vibrant green color and mild flavor. Choose firm pods without blemishes for optimal taste.

Red Okra:

A visually striking variety with a deep red hue. While the taste is similar to green okra, the color can add a unique aesthetic to your soup.

Clemson Spineless Okra:

Recognized for its lack of spines, making it easy to handle. It has a tender texture and is widely available.

Baby Okra:

Harvested when young for a more delicate texture. Baby okra is perfect for those who prefer a softer bite.

B. Tips on Selecting and Storing Fresh Okra

Appearance:

Choose okra pods that are firm, brightly colored, and free from blemishes. Avoid any pods that appear overly mature or tough.

Size Matters:

Smaller okra pods are generally more tender, while larger ones may be more fibrous. Select based on your preference for texture.

Storing Fresh Okra:

Store fresh okra in the refrigerator in a perforated plastic bag. Ensure they remain dry to prevent spoilage.

Use It Promptly:

Okra is best used within a few days of purchase for optimal freshness and flavor.

C. Adapting the Recipe to Seasonal Ingredients

Spring:

Embrace the vibrancy of spring by incorporating seasonal greens like spinach or young kale into the soup.

Summer:

Utilize fresh, ripe tomatoes during the summer months for a burst of sweetness and acidity in your soup.

Fall:

Experiment with hearty root vegetables such as carrots or sweet potatoes to add depth to the soup during the fall season.

Winter:

Consider adding winter squash, like butternut or acorn squash, for a comforting and seasonal twist.

Adapting the Okra Soup recipe to include seasonal ingredients allows you to take advantage of the freshest produce, enhancing the overall flavor and nutritional profile of your dish.

Chapter (11) Cultural Significance and Rituals

A. Okra Soup in Different Culinary Traditions

West African Cuisine:

In West Africa, Okra Soup holds deep cultural roots and is often considered a comfort food. It varies across regions, with each community infusing its unique flavors and ingredients.

Southern United States:

Okra is a staple in Southern cuisine, where dishes like gumbo showcase its versatility. Okra Soup, with its rich flavors, has found a home in Southern kitchens as a soul-warming dish.

Caribbean Influences:

Caribbean cuisines often incorporate okra in soups and stews, adding a Caribbean flair with spices and tropical ingredients.

B. Celebratory and Ritualistic Aspects

Festivals and Gatherings:

Okra Soup is often featured in festivals and celebratory gatherings, symbolizing abundance and community.

Symbolism of Okra:

In some cultures, okra is considered a symbol of fertility and prosperity, making Okra Soup a popular dish during significant life events.

Rituals and Traditions:

Okra Soup is sometimes prepared as part of rituals or traditions, particularly during important ceremonies or rites of passage.

C. Stories and Anecdotes from Okra Enthusiasts

Family Recipes Passed Down:

Many enthusiasts share stories of cherished family recipes, passed down through generations, creating a sense of continuity and connection.

Okra Soup Gatherings:

Some communities organize Okra Soup gatherings, where individuals share their variations of the dish, creating a sense of culinary camaraderie.

Global Okra Lovers:

Okra Soup enthusiasts around the world share anecdotes about discovering this dish, forming an international community bound by a love for its unique flavors.

The cultural significance and rituals surrounding Okra Soup highlight its role as not just a culinary creation but a symbol of community, tradition, and shared stories.

Chapter (12) Enhancing Flavors with Condiments

A. Hot Sauces and Pepper Blends

Traditional Pepper Sauces:

Explore traditional pepper sauces from different regions, such as West African pepper sauces or Southern-style hot sauces, to add a fiery kick to your Okra Soup.

Homemade Pepper Blends:

Create your pepper blend by combining fresh chilies, garlic, and a touch of vinegar. Adjust the spice level to your preference.

B. Pickled Vegetables and Relishes

Pickled Okra:

Enhance the okra flavor by adding pickled okra as a garnish. The tangy notes add a delightful contrast to the rich soup.

Cucumber Relish:

Prepare a cucumber relish with vinegar, sugar, and dill. The crispness of cucumbers and the tangy relish complement the soup's hearty nature.

C. Unique Condiment Combinations for Okra Soup

Coconut Sambal:

Elevate the soup with a coconut sambal made from grated coconut, lime juice, and chili. This tropical addition adds a refreshing twist.

Herb-infused Olive Oil:

Drizzle herb-infused olive oil over the soup just before serving. Combine olive oil with chopped herbs like rosemary, thyme, or basil for an extra layer of flavor.

Sour Cream and Chives:

For a creamy finish, top the soup with a dollop of sour cream and a sprinkle of fresh chives. The coolness balances the warmth of the dish.

Citrus Zest Blend:

Create a zesty citrus blend by mixing lemon and lime zest with a touch of sea salt. Sprinkle this over the soup for a burst of citrusy freshness.

Experimenting with different condiments allows you to tailor the Okra Soup to your taste preferences. These additions not only enhance the flavors but also provide a customizable element to the dining experience.

Chapter (13) Gluten-Free and Allergen-Friendly Adaptations

A. Substituting Ingredients for Gluten-Free Options

Flour Alternatives:

Substitute traditional wheat flour with gluten-free alternatives such as rice flour, almond flour, or a gluten-free all-purpose flour blend for thickening the soup.

Gluten-Free Broth:

Ensure the broth or stock used in the soup is gluten-free. Read labels carefully, as some commercial broths may contain gluten.

Rice or Quinoa Instead of Wheat-Based Side Dishes:

Offer gluten-free side dish options like rice, quinoa, or gluten-free bread to accommodate those with gluten sensitivities.

B. Allergy-Friendly Modifications for Common Allergens

Dairy-Free Options:

Use dairy-free alternatives like coconut milk or almond milk instead of traditional dairy products. Skip dairy-based garnishes for those with lactose intolerance or dairy allergies.

Nut-Free Substitutions:

Avoid nuts or nut-based condiments if there are nut allergies. Opt for alternative ingredients or omit them entirely.

Soy-Free Choices:

Choose soy-free alternatives for soy sauce or other soy-based products. Tamari, a gluten-free soy sauce, can be used as a substitute.

Egg-Free Considerations:

If an egg allergy is a concern, be mindful of hidden egg ingredients in condiments or marinades. Choose egg-free alternatives when applicable.

C. Ensuring Inclusivity in Okra Soup Preparation

Communicate Dietary Restrictions:

When preparing Okra Soup for a group, communicate with guests to understand and accommodate their dietary restrictions or allergies.

Labeling Ingredients:

If serving the soup at a gathering, provide ingredient labels to make it easy for individuals to identify potential allergens.

Flexible Condiment Bar:

Consider setting up a condiment bar with various gluten-free and allergy-friendly toppings, allowing individuals to customize their bowls.

By making simple substitutions and being mindful of common allergens, you can ensure that Okra Soup remains a delightful and inclusive dish for individuals with diverse dietary needs.

Chapter (14) Cooking with Kids

A. Family-Friendly Okra Soup Variations

Kid-Friendly Broth:

Opt for a mild broth base to cater to children's taste preferences. Vegetable or chicken broth with mild seasoning works well.

Colorful Vegetable Additions:

Include colorful vegetables like carrots, bell peppers, or sweet potatoes to make the soup visually appealing and enticing for kids.

Mini Meatballs:

Shape small, kid-friendly meatballs from ground chicken or turkey. Children can enjoy the fun of making and eating these bite-sized additions.

B. Engaging Children in the Kitchen

Slicing and Dicing:

Allow children to participate in safe slicing and dicing of vegetables under supervision. Use child-friendly knives for added safety.

Okra Preparation:

Engage kids in the process of cleaning and slicing okra. Teach them the techniques to reduce sliminess.

Meat Marinating:

Let kids participate in the marinating process. Provide a variety of kid-friendly marinade ingredients and let them mix and match flavors.

Soup Stirring:

Once the ingredients are in the pot, let children take turns stirring the soup. This simple task fosters a sense of involvement.

C. Educational Aspects of Okra Soup-Making

Learning About Ingredients:

Take the opportunity to teach kids about the different ingredients used in Okra Soup, their origins, and nutritional benefits.

Cultural Exploration:

Explore the cultural significance of Okra Soup. Share stories about how it's prepared in various parts of the world.

Math and Measurement:

Involve kids in measuring ingredients. Use the cooking process as a fun way to reinforce math skills.

Science of Cooking:

Explain the science behind cooking, such as how heat transforms ingredients and the role of different components in creating flavors.

Cooking Okra Soup with kids not only introduces them to the joy of preparing delicious meals but also provides valuable lessons in various subjects. The hands-on experience creates lasting memories and fosters a love for cooking.

Chapter (15) Okra Soup as Comfort Food

A. The Psychology of Comfort Food

Emotional Connection:

Comfort foods, like Okra Soup, often have a strong emotional connection. They provide a sense of familiarity and warmth, evoking positive feelings and memories.

Culinary Comfort:

The combination of rich flavors, hearty ingredients, and aromatic spices in Okra Soup contributes to its status as a culinary comfort, offering solace in times of need.

B. Personalizing Okra Soup for Comfort

Addition of Childhood Favorites:

Incorporate ingredients that hold personal significance or evoke fond childhood memories. This could be a particular spice, herb, or even a favorite vegetable.

Tailoring Seasonings:

Adjust the seasonings to match individual preferences, creating a personalized flavor profile that brings comfort and satisfaction.

Customizing Texture:

Consider blending a portion of the soup for a creamier texture or leaving it chunky for those who prefer a heartier experience.

C. Nostalgic Okra Soup Recipes from Childhood

Family Heirloom Recipes:

Share stories of family recipes passed down through generations. These recipes often carry a sense of nostalgia and comfort.

Childhood Favorites Remade:

Recreate Okra Soup recipes enjoyed during childhood, adding a touch of creativity or a modern twist to make them uniquely yours.

Cooking with Loved Ones:

Involve loved ones in the cooking process. The shared experience of preparing and enjoying Okra Soup together enhances the comforting aspect of the meal.

Okra Soup, with its comforting qualities, becomes more than just a dish – it transforms into a source of solace and connection, reminding us of the warmth and love associated with home-cooked meals.

Chapter (16) Showcasing Okra in Modern Gastronomy

A. Okra Soup Fusion with Global Cuisines

Asian-Inspired Fusion:

Infuse Okra Soup with Asian flavors by adding ingredients like lemongrass, ginger, and soy sauce. This fusion brings a unique twist to the traditional recipe.

Mediterranean Elegance:

Elevate Okra Soup with Mediterranean influences by incorporating ingredients such as olives, capers, and a drizzle of extra virgin olive oil.

Latin American Flair:

Add a touch of Latin American vibrancy with ingredients like cilantro, lime, and a hint of spice. Consider serving the soup with a side of avocado salsa.

B. Okra Soup Trends in Contemporary Restaurants

Gourmet Presentations:

Contemporary restaurants often showcase Okra Soup with gourmet presentations, emphasizing aesthetic appeal through creative plating techniques.

Deconstructed Versions:

Some chefs experiment with deconstructed Okra Soup, presenting elements separately to highlight each component's distinct flavor and texture.

Artisanal Broths:

Emphasize the use of artisanal broths, made in-house with carefully selected ingredients, to elevate the overall quality and depth of the soup.

C. Elevating Okra Soup for Special Occasions

Truffle Infusion:

Elevate Okra Soup for special occasions by infusing truffle oil or truffle essence, adding a luxurious and earthy undertone to the dish.

Seafood Extravaganza:

Create a special seafood edition of Okra Soup by adding shrimp, crab, or other seafood delicacies. This indulgent version is perfect for celebratory meals.

Interactive Dining Experience:

Offer an interactive dining experience by serving Okra Soup in individual pots or bowls, allowing guests to customize their additions and toppings.

Showcasing Okra Soup in modern gastronomy involves experimenting with global flavors, incorporating contemporary trends from fine dining establishments, and elevating the dish to create a memorable experience for special occasions.

Chapter (17) Health Benefits of Okra

A. Nutritional Profile of Okra

Rich in Fiber:

Okra is an excellent source of dietary fiber, promoting digestive health and aiding in maintaining a healthy weight.

Vitamins and Minerals:

Packed with essential vitamins and minerals, including vitamin C, vitamin K, folate, and magnesium, which contribute to overall well-being.

Low-Calorie Superfood:

Okra is low in calories but high in nutrients, making it a nutrient-dense addition to your diet.

B. Okra's Medicinal Properties

Blood Sugar Regulation:

The soluble fiber in okra helps regulate blood sugar levels, making it beneficial for individuals with diabetes or those at risk.

Heart Health:

Okra contains potassium and antioxidants, contributing to heart health by promoting healthy blood pressure and reducing oxidative stress.

Anti-Inflammatory Effects:

The presence of anti-inflammatory compounds in okra may help alleviate inflammation in the body, contributing to overall health.

Improving Digestive Health:

The fiber content in okra supports a healthy digestive system, preventing constipation and promoting regular bowel movements.

C. Creating a Balanced and Nutrient-Rich Okra Soup

Incorporate a Variety of Vegetables:

Enhance the nutritional content of Okra Soup by including a diverse range of vegetables. This adds vitamins, minerals, and antioxidants to the dish.

Lean Protein Choices:

Choose lean protein sources such as chicken or turkey to maintain a balanced and nutritious profile.

Use Whole Grains:

If including grains, opt for whole grains like brown rice or quinoa to boost fiber content and provide sustained energy.

Limit Added Fats:

While fats are essential, be mindful of added fats. Opt for healthier fats like olive oil and control portions for a balanced approach.

By understanding the nutritional benefits of okra and crafting a well-balanced Okra Soup, you not only create a delicious meal but also promote health and well-being through wholesome and nourishing ingredients.

Chapter (18) Okra Soup Challenges and Solutions

A. Addressing Common Cooking Issues

Sliminess Concerns:

Issue: Okra can become slimy when cooked.

Solution: Pre-soak okra in vinegar or lemon juice, roast or sear it before adding to the soup, and incorporate acidic ingredients like tomatoes to minimize sliminess.

Overcooking Meats:

Issue: Meats becoming tough due to overcooking.

Solution: Adjust cooking times based on meat cuts and choose cooking methods that suit the chosen protein, ensuring meats are tender and flavorful.

B. Troubleshooting for Texture and Flavor

Bland Flavor Profile:

Issue: The soup lacks depth of flavor.

Solution: Experiment with additional spices, herbs, and flavor enhancers. Adjust salt levels and consider incorporating umami-rich ingredients like soy sauce or Worcestershire sauce.

Inconsistent Texture:

Issue: Inconsistencies in the texture of vegetables or meats.

Solution: Ensure uniform slicing and chopping. Consider adjusting cooking times for ingredients that may require different durations.

C. Expert Tips for Overcoming Challenges

Professional Chef Insight:

Tip: Chef's tip for reducing sliminess is to blanch okra in boiling water for a few minutes before incorporating it into the soup. This technique helps maintain its vibrant color while minimizing unwanted texture.

Balancing Flavors:

Tip: To achieve a well-balanced flavor, taste the soup throughout the cooking process and adjust seasonings gradually. This prevents over-seasoning and allows for precise flavor control.

Layered Cooking:

Tip: Practice layered cooking by adding ingredients at different stages to build complexity. Start with aromatics, progress to meats, and finish with delicate items like fresh herbs to maximize flavor infusion.

Addressing challenges in Okra Soup not only ensures a delicious outcome but also enhances your culinary skills. Utilize these solutions and expert tips to create a consistently enjoyable Okra Soup experience.

Chapter (19) Okra Desserts and Sweets

A. Surprising Sweet Treats Using Okra

Okra Jelly:

Create a unique and vibrant okra jelly by blending okra with sugar and lemon juice. This jelly can be used as a spread, topping, or filling for desserts.

Okra-Pineapple Sorbet:

Blend okra with pineapple and a touch of honey to make a refreshing sorbet. This unexpected combination offers a delightful and healthy dessert option.

B. Okra-Based Dessert Innovations

Okra Chocolate Brownies:

Incorporate finely grated okra into your favorite brownie recipe. The okra adds moisture and a subtle nuttiness, creating a healthier twist to this classic dessert.

Okra Panna Cotta:

Infuse the creamy texture of panna cotta with okra essence. Blend cooked and strained okra into the cream mixture before setting for a unique and silky dessert.

C. Dessert Pairings with Okra Soup

Citrus Okra Soup with Fruit Salad:

Complement a citrus-infused Okra Soup with a refreshing fruit salad. The contrast of warm soup and cool, sweet fruits creates a delightful balance.

Okra Soup Parfait:

Layer small glasses with Okra Soup, followed by a dollop of yogurt or coconut cream, and a sprinkle of granola. This parfait offers a satisfying mix of flavors and textures.

Okra Soup-Spiced Cakes:

Infuse cakes or muffins with the spices and flavors found in Okra Soup. This creates a harmonious pairing, making dessert an extension of the savory meal.

Incorporating okra into desserts opens up a world of possibilities, adding a surprising twist to familiar treats. These sweet innovations can be enjoyed on their own or paired creatively with Okra Soup for a complete culinary experience.

Chapter (20) Okra Soup in Festivals and Gatherings

A. Okra Soup as a Festive Dish

Celebrating Diversity:

Okra Soup's versatility makes it an ideal dish for festivals, embracing various ingredients and flavors that reflect the diversity of culinary traditions.

Symbolism of Abundance:

Okra Soup, with its rich and hearty ingredients, symbolizes abundance and communal sharing, making it fitting for festive occasions.

B. Catering Tips for Large Gatherings

Preparation and Planning:

Plan ahead by prepping ingredients, marinating meats, and creating a cooking schedule. This ensures a smooth cooking process, especially when catering for large groups.

Buffet-Style Service:

Opt for a buffet-style setup to accommodate diverse tastes. Provide separate bowls of condiments, side dishes, and variations to allow guests to customize their Okra Soup experience.

Maintaining Warmth:

Use chafing dishes or slow cookers to maintain the soup's warmth throughout the event. This ensures that guests can enjoy a comforting bowl of Okra Soup at their convenience.

C. Creating a Memorable Okra Soup Experience

Live Cooking Stations:

Incorporate live cooking stations where guests can witness the Okra Soup preparation. This interactive experience adds an element of excitement and engagement.

Decorative Presentation:

Elevate the visual appeal of Okra Soup by serving it in decorative bowls or hollowed-out bread bowls. Garnish with fresh herbs or edible flowers for a festive touch.

Themed Variations:

Introduce themed Okra Soup variations based on the festival or gathering's theme. This allows for creativity and customization, making the dish even more memorable.

Okra Soup in festivals and gatherings provides an opportunity to celebrate culinary diversity and create lasting memories. By applying catering tips and enhancing the overall experience, you ensure that Okra Soup becomes a centerpiece for communal joy.

Chapter (21) Gardening Tips for Homegrown Okra

A. Cultivating Okra in Home Gardens

Choosing Okra Varieties:

Select okra varieties suitable for your climate and garden space. Clemson Spineless and Burgundy are popular choices for home gardens.

Optimal Planting Conditions:

Plant okra in well-drained soil with plenty of sunlight. Ensure proper spacing between plants to promote air circulation and prevent disease.

Companion Planting:

Plant okra alongside compatible companions such as basil, marigolds, or peppers. These plants can provide natural pest control and enhance overall growth.

B. Harvesting and Preserving Fresh Okra

Harvesting Techniques:

Harvest okra pods when they are 3-4 inches long for optimal tenderness. Use sharp scissors or pruning shears to avoid damaging the plant.

Preserving Freshness:

Store freshly harvested okra in the refrigerator for up to a week. To extend freshness, wrap the pods in a damp cloth or store them in perforated plastic bags.

Freezing for Future Use:

If you have a surplus of okra, blanch the pods before freezing. This preserves their quality, allowing you to enjoy homegrown okra in Okra Soup throughout the year.

C. Farm-to-Table Okra Soup Experience

Direct Harvest for Meals:

Harvest okra directly from your garden just before preparing Okra Soup. This farm-to-table approach ensures maximum freshness and flavor.

Seasonal Variations:

Embrace seasonal variations in your Okra Soup by incorporating other garden-fresh vegetables and herbs. This adds a dynamic and ever-changing aspect to your homegrown culinary creations.

Sharing Homegrown Bounty:

Share the joy of homegrown okra by serving Okra Soup to friends and family. This farm-to-table experience creates a connection between your garden and the dining table.

Cultivating and using homegrown okra in Okra Soup enhances the overall culinary experience, providing a sense of satisfaction and pride in creating a dish from seed to table.

Chapter (22) Okra Art and Presentation

A. Creative Plating Techniques

Colorful Contrasts:

Arrange okra slices, vibrant vegetables, and meats to create a visually appealing contrast of colors on the plate. This enhances the overall presentation of Okra Soup.

Edible Garnishes:

Utilize edible garnishes like fresh herbs, microgreens, or edible flowers to add a touch of elegance. These elements not only enhance the visual appeal but also contribute to the flavor profile.

Bread Bowl Magic:

Serve Okra Soup in hollowed-out bread bowls for a rustic and inviting presentation. This not only adds a creative touch but also allows for an interactive dining experience.

B. Food Photography Tips for Okra Soup

Natural Lighting:

Capture the beauty of Okra Soup using natural light. Place the dish near a window or outdoors to showcase its colors and textures effectively.

Close-Up Shots:

Zoom in to capture the intricate details of okra slices, meat, and herbs. Close-up shots highlight the richness and depth of the soup.

Capturing Steam:

Take photos while the soup is still steaming to convey warmth and freshness. The rising steam adds a dynamic element to your food photography.

C. Okra-Inspired Artistic Culinary Creations

Okra Mandala:

Arrange okra slices in a circular pattern on the soup's surface, creating an intricate mandala. This artistic touch adds a unique flair to the presentation.

Okra Soup Mosaics:

Experiment with arranging different ingredients in mosaic patterns on the plate. Use colorful vegetables, meats, and okra to create visually stunning culinary art.

Abstract Okra Paintings:

Play with swirls of vibrant okra soup on the plate to create abstract paintings. Use the natural colors of the ingredients to evoke a sense of artistry in your presentation.

By incorporating creative plating techniques, mastering food photography skills, and experimenting with artistic culinary creations, you can transform Okra Soup into a visually stunning masterpiece that engages the senses.

Chapter (23) Okra Soup and Sustainability

A. Sustainable Sourcing of Ingredients

Local and Seasonal Produce:

Prioritize using locally sourced and seasonal ingredients for Okra Soup. This supports local farmers, reduces transportation emissions, and ensures freshness.

Ethical Meat Choices:

Opt for ethically sourced and sustainably raised meats. Look for certifications that indicate humane and environmentally conscious practices in meat production.

Organic and Non-GMO Options:

Choose organic and non-GMO ingredients when possible. This helps promote sustainable farming practices and reduces the environmental impact of agricultural chemicals.

B. Reducing Food Waste in Okra Soup Preparation

Creative Uses for Scraps:

Utilize okra trimmings, vegetable peels, and meat bones to make homemade broth. This minimizes waste while adding depth of flavor to your Okra Soup.

Freezing Excess Ingredients:

If you have surplus okra or other ingredients, freeze them for future use. This not only reduces food waste but also ensures a ready supply of fresh ingredients for your next batch of Okra Soup.

Composting:

Compost vegetable scraps and other organic waste from Okra Soup preparation. This contributes to nutrient-rich soil for gardening or local community initiatives.

C. Eco-Friendly Practices for Okra Enthusiasts

Reusable and Eco-Friendly Kitchen Tools:

Invest in reusable and sustainable kitchen tools, such as bamboo cutting boards, stainless steel utensils, and silicone storage containers.

Water Conservation:

Practice water-efficient cooking by reusing water from washing vegetables for watering plants. This small adjustment contributes to sustainable kitchen practices.

Zero-Waste Cooking Classes:

Host or attend cooking classes focused on zero-waste cooking. Learn and share techniques for using every part of ingredients, including okra, to minimize waste.

Embracing sustainability in Okra Soup preparation not only benefits the environment but also promotes a mindful and responsible approach to cooking. By sourcing ingredients responsibly and minimizing waste, you contribute to a more sustainable and eco-friendly culinary experience.

Chapter (24) Okra Soup Cook-Offs and Competitions

A. Organizing and Participating in Okra Soup Challenges

Event Planning:

Organize Okra Soup cook-offs as community events, encouraging participants to showcase their creativity and culinary skills. Consider themed competitions to add excitement.

Community Involvement:

Engage local chefs, home cooks, and culinary enthusiasts to participate in Okra Soup challenges. Create a sense of community and camaraderie around this beloved dish.

Online Competitions:

Extend the reach of Okra Soup competitions by organizing online events. Participants can share their recipes, cooking processes, and final creations virtually.

B. Judging Criteria and Tips

Flavor Complexity:

Judges should evaluate the Okra Soup based on the depth and complexity of flavors. A well-balanced combination of spices, herbs, and ingredients enhances the overall taste.

Texture and Consistency:

Assess the soup's texture, ensuring a harmonious blend of tender meats, well-prepared okra, and other ingredients. Consistency should be neither too thick nor too thin.

Presentation Creativity:

Place emphasis on creative plating and presentation. Judges can consider how well the Okra Soup visually appeals to the audience and showcases the cook's artistic flair.

Innovation and Uniqueness:

Acknowledge contestants who bring innovation to Okra Soup preparation. This could include unique flavor combinations, inventive ingredient choices, or creative twists on traditional recipes.

C. Celebrating Okra Soup Excellence

Awards and Recognition:

Award winners with certificates, trophies, or culinary-themed prizes to celebrate their Okra Soup excellence. Recognize achievements in various categories, such as Best Flavor, Most Creative Presentation, or Judges' Choice.

Community Tastings:

Extend the celebration beyond participants by organizing community tastings. Allow attendees to sample and enjoy the diverse Okra Soup creations, fostering a sense of community and appreciation for culinary talent.

Cookbook Compilation:

Compile a cookbook featuring the winning Okra Soup recipes along with participants' contributions. This serves as a lasting memento and inspiration for future Okra Soup enthusiasts.

Okra Soup cook-offs and competitions provide a platform for culinary enthusiasts to showcase their skills, celebrate creativity, and foster a sense of community. By organizing and participating in such events, you contribute to the culinary richness of the community.

Chapter (25) Future Trends in Okra Cuisine

A. Emerging Okra Soup Trends

Global Fusion Variations:

Anticipate the emergence of global fusion Okra Soups, blending diverse culinary traditions and flavors. Expect to see innovative combinations inspired by international cuisines.

Health and Wellness Focus:

Future Okra Soups may place a stronger emphasis on health and wellness, incorporating superfoods, functional ingredients, and mindful cooking techniques to cater to health-conscious consumers.

Plant-Based and Vegan Options:

With the growing popularity of plant-based diets, anticipate a surge in creative plant-based and vegan Okra Soup variations. Chefs and home cooks will experiment with alternative protein sources and plant-powered flavor enhancers.

B. Culinary Innovations and Experiments

Okra-Centric Menus:

Envision restaurants and home chefs curating entire menus centered around okra, featuring diverse dishes beyond soup. This trend may highlight okra's versatility and potential in various culinary applications.

Okra-Paired Beverages:

Experimentation with okra-infused beverages, such as mocktails or teas, might become a trend. These innovative pairings could offer unique flavors and elevate the overall dining experience.

Tech-Driven Cooking:

Anticipate the integration of technology in Okra Soup preparation, with the use of smart kitchen appliances, augmented reality (AR) cooking tutorials, and personalized recipe recommendations based on individual preferences.

C. Envisioning the Future of Okra-Based Dishes

Okra Dessert Revolution:

Imagine a future where okra is celebrated in a wide array of desserts, from cakes and pastries to ice creams. The versatility of okra could inspire a dessert revolution, challenging traditional sweet norms.

Interactive Cooking Experiences:

Future cooking experiences may involve virtual reality (VR) or augmented reality (AR) platforms, allowing users to virtually engage in the process of selecting, preparing, and enjoying Okra Soup from the comfort of their homes.

Sustainable Okra Practices:

In line with broader sustainability trends, foresee increased focus on sustainable okra cultivation, with home gardeners and farmers adopting eco-friendly practices to minimize the environmental impact of okra production.

The future of Okra Cuisine holds exciting possibilities, from innovative soup variations to culinary experiments that push the boundaries of traditional cooking. Embracing emerging trends ensures a dynamic and ever-evolving okra culinary landscape.

Chapter (26) Okra Soup and Cultural Celebrations

A. Okra Soup in Festivals and Holidays
Festival Feasts:

During cultural festivals and holidays, Okra Soup takes center stage in celebratory feasts. It symbolizes togetherness, abundance, and the joy of sharing a delicious meal with loved ones.

Seasonal Significance:

Okra Soup often aligns with specific seasons and harvest periods. Its inclusion in festive menus reflects the seasonal availability of fresh ingredients and adds a touch of tradition to the celebration.

B. Traditional Okra Soup Rituals
Ceremonial Preparations:

In some cultures, the preparation of Okra Soup is a ceremonial event. Families gather to participate in the cooking process, passing down traditional recipes and techniques from one generation to the next.

Symbolism in Ingredients:

Each ingredient in Okra Soup may hold cultural significance. For example, certain vegetables or spices could symbolize prosperity, good luck, or the essence of a particular celebration.

C. Crafting Okra Soup Menus for Special Occasions
Multi-Course Okra Menus:

Elevate Okra Soup for special occasions by crafting multi-course menus. Start with a refreshing okra-inspired appetizer, progress to the main Okra Soup dish, and conclude with a unique okra-infused dessert.

Customization for Events:

Customize Okra Soup menus based on the cultural significance of the event. Consider incorporating specific ingredients, flavors, or cooking techniques that align with the traditions of the celebration.

Pairing with Traditional Dishes:

Integrate Okra Soup seamlessly with other traditional dishes served during cultural celebrations. This creates a cohesive and harmonious menu that honors culinary heritage.

Okra Soup becomes more than just a dish during cultural celebrations; it transforms into a symbol of cultural identity, shared memories, and the richness of tradition. Crafting special menus and observing traditional rituals enhances the overall cultural experience associated with Okra Soup.

Chapter (27) Okra Soup and Wine Pairings

A. Selecting Wines to Complement Okra Soup

Light and Crisp Whites:

Choose light and crisp white wines, such as Sauvignon Blanc or Pinot Grigio, to complement the freshness of Okra Soup. The acidity in these wines harmonizes well with the vibrant flavors of the soup.

Unoaked Chardonnay:

An unoaked Chardonnay provides a balanced option with its crispness and hints of citrus. Its subtle notes enhance the overall dining experience without overpowering the delicate flavors of Okra Soup.

Rosé Elegance:

Opt for a dry rosé with floral and fruity notes. The versatility of rosé complements both the okra's earthiness and the savory elements in the soup.

B. Wine Varieties for Different Meat Choices

Chicken and White Wine:

Pair Okra Soup with chicken with a light to medium-bodied white wine. Chardonnay or a Viognier complements the chicken's flavors without overshadowing the soup's subtleties.

Beef and Red Blend:

For Okra Soup with beef, consider a medium to full-bodied red blend like Merlot or a red Zinfandel. The rich, savory notes in the wine complement the heartiness of the beef.

Lamb and Syrah/Shiraz:

Opt for a Syrah or Shiraz when pairing Okra Soup with lamb. The bold and spicy characteristics of these wines enhance the robust flavor of lamb in the soup.

C. Enhancing the Dining Experience with Wine

Tasting Notes Exploration:

Encourage diners to explore the tasting notes of the chosen wine alongside Okra Soup. Discuss how the wine's characteristics interact with the flavors in the soup for a more immersive dining experience.

Wine and Soup Pairing Events:

Host special wine and Okra Soup pairing events where enthusiasts can sample different wine varieties alongside variations of Okra Soup. This allows for an interactive and educational experience.

Customized Wine Flights:

Create customized wine flights to accompany Okra Soup. This allows diners to savor a variety of wines, each chosen to complement specific elements of the soup.

Pairing Okra Soup with the right wines enhances the overall dining experience, bringing out the best in both the dish and the chosen wines. The careful selection of wine varieties ensures a harmonious and delightful combination for enthusiasts to enjoy.

Chapter (28) Okra Soup for Quick Weeknight Dinners

A. Time-Efficient Okra Soup Recipes

Quick Chicken and Okra Soup:

Use boneless, skinless chicken thighs for a faster cooking time. Sauté aromatics, add sliced okra, diced chicken, and quickly simmer in a pre-made broth for a speedy and satisfying soup.

Speedy Vegetarian Okra Soup:

Skip the meat preparation and opt for a vegetarian version with pre-cut okra, canned tomatoes, and ready-to-use vegetable broth. This reduces cooking time while maintaining a wholesome flavor.

Instant Pot Okra Soup:

Utilize the Instant Pot for a quick cooking method. Sauté aromatics, add ingredients, and pressure-cook for a fraction of the time. This method ensures a flavorful Okra Soup in a hurry.

B. One-Pot Okra Soup Solutions

Effortless Beef and Okra One-Pot:

Brown beef in the same pot used for the soup, minimizing cleanup. Combine vegetables, broth, and spices, allowing them to simmer together for a convenient one-pot meal.

All-in-One Seafood Okra Stew:

Create a seafood-inspired Okra Soup using a single pot. Combine shrimp, fish, or other seafood with okra, tomatoes, and seasonings, streamlining the cooking process.

Quick and Easy Vegan Okra Stew:

Craft a vegan Okra Soup using a single pot. Combine sliced okra, beans, tomatoes, and a variety of vegetables for a nutritious and time-efficient weeknight dinner.

C. Planning and Prep Tips for Busy Weeknights

Pre-Cut Ingredients:

Pre-cut okra, vegetables, and meat on the weekends. Store them in separate containers for quick assembly during busy weeknights.

Batch Cooking:

Prepare a larger batch of Okra Soup during the weekend and portion it for the week. Reheat single servings for a quick and hearty dinner.

Frozen Okra Convenience:

Keep a bag of frozen okra on hand for last-minute Okra Soup preparations. Frozen okra cooks quickly and retains its freshness, making it a convenient option.

Okra Soup for quick weeknight dinners is achievable with strategic recipes, one-pot solutions, and efficient planning. These time-saving techniques ensure a delicious and nourishing meal even on the busiest evenings.

Chapter (29) Okra Soup as a Culinary Canvas

A. Artistic Garnishing Techniques

Herb Swirls and Spirals:

Elevate the visual appeal of Okra Soup by incorporating delicate herb swirls or spirals on the surface. Use fresh herbs like parsley or cilantro to create artistic patterns.

Edible Flower Petals:

Delight the senses with the addition of edible flower petals as a garnish. Choose vibrant and colorful edible flowers to add a touch of elegance to your Okra Soup.

Spice Dust Designs:

Experiment with spice dustings to create intricate designs on the soup's surface. Use ground spices like paprika or turmeric to add both flavor and visual appeal.

B. Colorful Presentation Ideas

Rainbow Vegetable Arrangement:

Arrange a variety of colorful vegetables around the edge of the serving bowl, creating a rainbow-like effect. This not only enhances the presentation but also offers a visual feast.

Layered Ingredients Showcase:

Display the layers of ingredients in the soup, showcasing the vibrant colors of okra, meats, and other vegetables. This transparent presentation adds depth and intrigue.

Contrasting Soup Bowls:

Choose contrasting-colored bowls to serve Okra Soup. The color interplay between the soup and the bowl enhances the overall visual impact and makes for an eye-catching presentation.

C. Encouraging Culinary Creativity with Okra Soup

Interactive Garnish Stations:

Set up an interactive garnish station during gatherings. Provide an array of herbs, spices, and edible flowers, allowing guests to personalize their Okra Soup with creative garnishes.

Themed Culinary Competitions:

Host themed Okra Soup garnishing competitions to encourage culinary creativity. Themes could range from seasonal inspirations to cultural influences, sparking participants' imagination.

Photography and Social Media Challenges:

Encourage enthusiasts to share their creatively garnished Okra Soup on social media platforms. Create challenges with specific hashtags to foster a sense of community and inspiration.

Okra Soup is not just a dish; it's a canvas waiting to be adorned with artistic flair. By incorporating these garnishing techniques and presentation ideas, you transform Okra Soup into a culinary masterpiece that engages the senses and invites creative expression.

Chapter (30) Exploring Regional Okra Variations

A. Okra Soup Across Different Countries
West African Okra Stew (Gumbo):
Venture into West Africa, where Okra Soup takes the form of a rich stew known as Gumbo. Traditionally prepared with okra, meat, and a blend of spices, this variant showcases the deep culinary roots of the region.

Louisiana Creole Okra Gumbo:
Travel to the southern United States and savor the distinctive flavors of Louisiana Creole Okra Gumbo. A harmonious blend of French, African, and Spanish influences, this variant often features a roux, sausage, and a medley of local spices.

Middle Eastern Bamya:
Explore the Middle East with Bamya, a flavorful okra and meat stew. Often enriched with tomatoes, garlic, and a variety of aromatic spices, this rendition reflects the culinary diversity of the region.

B. Regional Spices and Flavors
Caribbean Calaloo:
Immerse yourself in the vibrant flavors of the Caribbean with Calaloo, a spinach and okra-based soup. Infused with Caribbean spices like Scotch bonnet peppers and thyme, Calaloo brings a burst of tropical warmth to the palate.

Indian Bhindi Masala:
Journey to India, where Bhindi Masala showcases okra's versatility. Sautéed with aromatic spices, tomatoes, and onions, this flavorful dish is a testament to the rich tapestry of Indian culinary traditions.

Asian-inspired Okra Stir-Fry:
Experience the simplicity and bold flavors of Asian cuisine with an Okra Stir-Fry. Quick-cooked with soy sauce, ginger, and garlic, this

variation demonstrates the art of balancing sweet, savory, and umami flavors.

C. Culinary Travelogue: A Tour of Okra Soup Delights

Okra Soup Tasting Events:

Host Okra Soup tasting events that take participants on a virtual tour of global variations. Share stories, traditions, and cooking techniques, allowing participants to savor the diversity of Okra Soup.

Cooking Classes with Guest Chefs:

Collaborate with guest chefs from different regions to conduct virtual cooking classes. Each chef can showcase their regional twist on Okra Soup, providing a hands-on experience for enthusiasts.

Okra Soup Cookbook Featuring Global Variations:

Compile a cookbook featuring Okra Soup recipes from around the world. This culinary travelogue celebrates the global diversity of Okra Soup and invites readers to embark on their own international Okra Soup adventures.

Embark on a culinary journey around the globe as you explore the regional variations of Okra Soup. Each variant tells a story of culture, tradition, and the unique spices that contribute to the global appeal of this beloved dish.

❖ Conclusion

A. Recap of the Okra Soup-Making Journey

Throughout this culinary exploration, we've delved into the vibrant world of Okra Soup, uncovering its rich history, diverse variations, and the artistry involved in its creation. From selecting fresh ingredients to mastering cooking techniques, every step contributes to the symphony of flavors that make Okra Soup a culinary delight.

We've navigated the nuances of preparing Okra Soup with succulent meat pieces, offering insights into everything from cleaning and slicing okra to selecting the perfect cuts of meat. The aromatic journey has taken us through sautéing aromatics, creating flavorful broths, and mastering the art of simmering for optimal fusion.

Accompanying side dishes, garnishing for presentation, and thoughtful beverage pairings have elevated Okra Soup into a complete dining experience. We explored variations, troubleshooted common issues, and shared tips and tricks to make your Okra Soup journey seamless.

B. Encouragement to Explore and Experiment

As you embark on your Okra Soup-making journey, remember that the kitchen is your canvas, and Okra Soup is your masterpiece. Feel free to experiment with flavors, explore regional twists, and adapt the recipe to your unique taste preferences.

Whether you're a seasoned chef or a novice in the kitchen, Okra Soup offers a canvas for creativity and a platform for culinary exploration. Don't hesitate to customize the recipe, introduce your own variations, and share the joy of Okra Soup with friends and family.

May your Okra Soup adventures be filled with delicious discoveries and delightful moments around the dining table. As you savor each spoonful, relish in the satisfaction of creating a dish that not only tantalizes the taste buds but also carries the warmth of tradition and the joy of culinary artistry.

Happy cooking, and may your Okra Soup always be a celebration of flavors, culture, and the joy of sharing a wonderful meal.

www.ingramcontent.com/pod-product-compliance
Lightning Source LLC
Chambersburg PA
CBHW051317160726
47994CB00003B/1493